Dear Parents,

Children's earliest experiences with stories and books usually involve grown-ups reading to them. However, reading should be active, and as adults, we can help young readers make meaning of the text by prompting them to relate the book to what they already know and to their personal experiences. Our questions will lead them to move beyond the simple story and pictures and encourage them to think beneath the surface. For example, after reading a story about the sleep habits of animals, you might ask, "Do you remember when you moved into a big bed? Could you see the moon out of your window?"

Illustrations in these books are wonderful and can be used in a variety of ways. Your questions about them can direct the child to details and encourage him or her to think about what those details tell us about the story. You might ask the child to find three different "beds" used by animals and insects in the book. Illustrations can even be used to inspire readers to draw their own pictures related to the text.

At the end of each book, there are some suggested questions and activities related to the story. These questions range in difficulty and will help you move young readers from the text itself to thinking skills such as comparing and contrasting, predicting, applying what they learned to new situations and identifying things they want to find out more about. This conversation about their reading may even result in the children becoming the storytellers, rather than simply the listeners!

Harriet Ziefert, M.A.
Language Arts/Reading Specialist

More to Think  About

Does a Bear Wear Boots?

Does a Beaver Sleep in a Bed?

Does a Camel Cook Spaghetti?

Does a Panda Go to School?

Does an Owl Wear Eyeglasses?

Does a Tiger Go to the Dentist?

Doe a Hippo Go to the Doctor?

Does a Seal Smile?

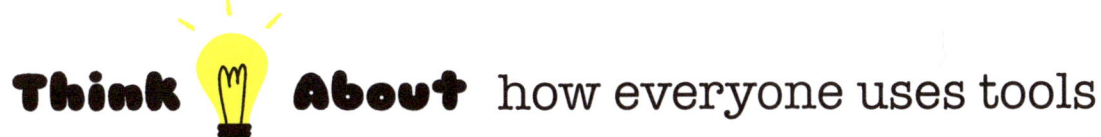

Think About how everyone uses tools

Does a Woodpecker Use a Hammer?

Harriet Ziefert • illustrations by Emily Bolam

BLUE APPLE

Text copyright © 2014 by Harriet Ziefert
Illustrations copyright © 2014 by Emily Bolam
All rights reserved
CIP data is available.
Published in the United States 2014 by
 Blue Apple Books
South Orange, New Jersey
www.blueapplebooks.com

Does a gull use a hammer?

Does a woodpecker use a hammer?

Not exactly.
What sounds like hammering is really the woodpecker using his bill to make holes in a tree trunk.

What does the woodpecker want?
Insects!
Juicy and delicious if you're a woodpecker.

Does a cow hammer?

No. A cow cannot use a hammer.

It has hooves—not paws—and it cannot hold a tool in its hooves.

A cow can kick with its hooves.
Sometimes it kicks over the milk bucket . . .
and sometimes the person who is milking!

You must be kidding! An octopus has eight arms, but none of them can hold a hammer.

An octopus has suckers on the ends of its arms.

The octopus uses the suckers to pick up pieces of shell. The shell pieces are needed for protection because the octopus is soft and squishy and has no hard body parts.

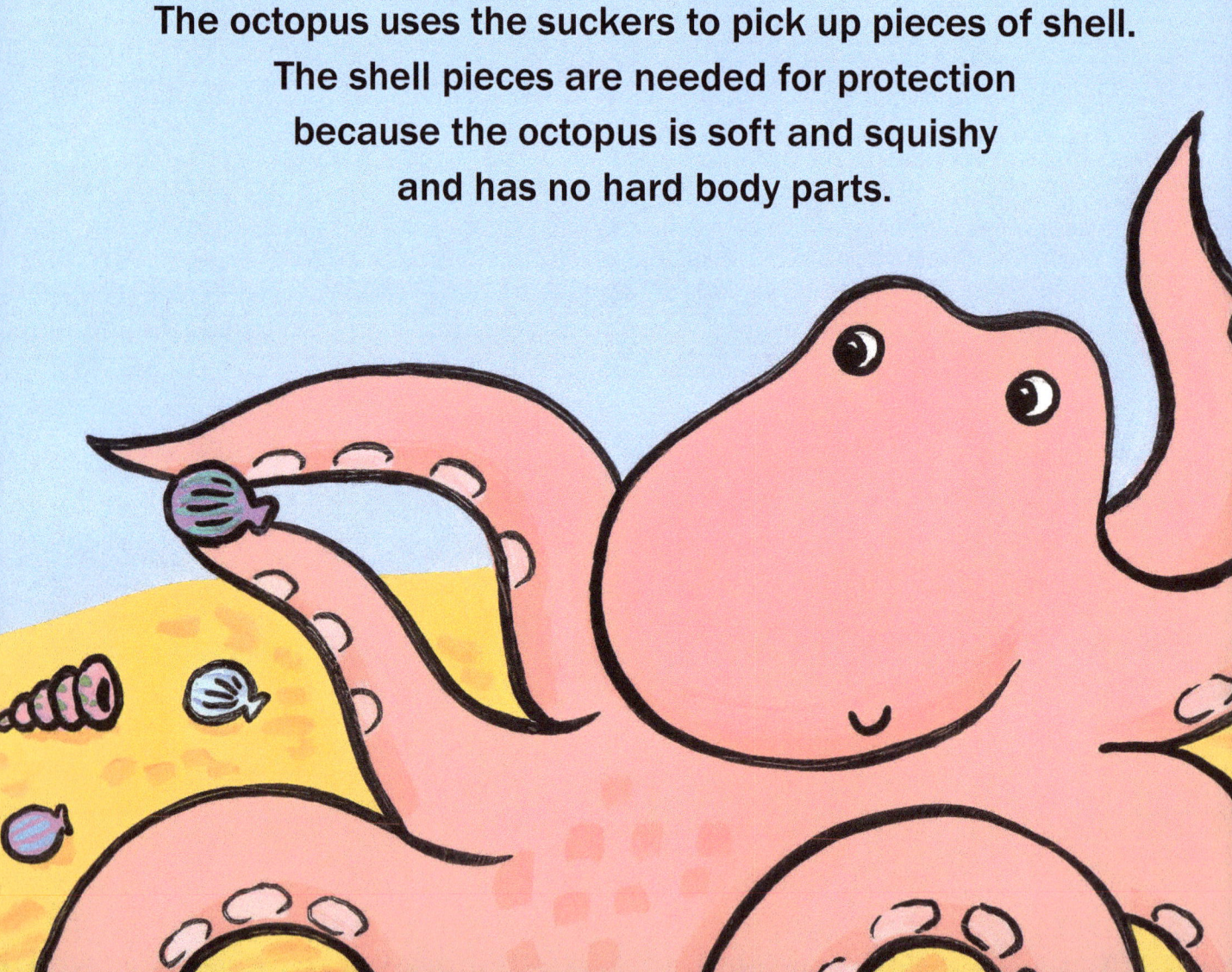

Does a gorilla hammer?

Not exactly!
But a few gorillas
have been seen using rocks
to smash open pine nuts.

A gorilla could use a hammer.
But it couldn't hold it very well.
And most important, a gorilla doesn't have
the brain power to design a hammer.
Or a screwdriver. Or a wrench.

Do *any* animals make tools?

A relative of the gorilla, the chimpanzee,
finds long sticks to put inside termite nests.
The chimp pulls out the termites and
eats them off the end of the stick—
as if they were marshmallows. Yum!

Can the chimp make a better termite grabber by putting two sticks together?
No. It cannot.
Only a person could make a better grabber.

But the most important tool invented by man was the wheel.

The wheel, along with the pulley and the screw, was used by ancient Egyptians to build the pyramids.

People use different hammers to do different jobs.

Look at the heads of these screwdrivers. Again, people use them for different purposes.

These screws and nails are all different, for different uses.

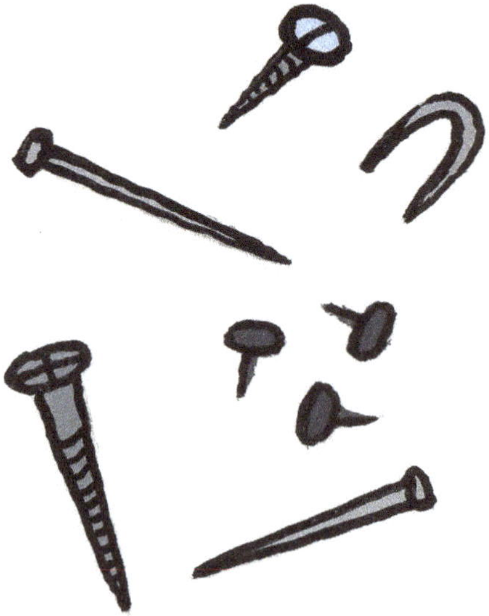

Think 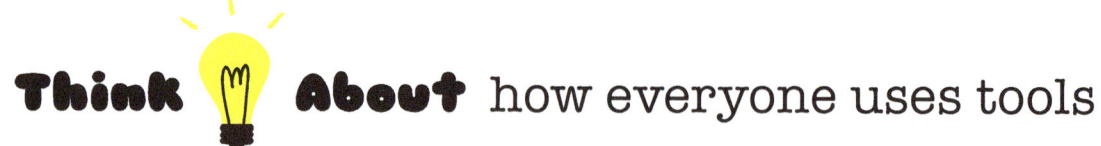 About how everyone uses tools

This book explains how animals such as the gorilla and the chimpanzee use tools differently from people.

Compare and Contrast

Eating is an important job for an animal or a person.

- How does a squirrel crack nuts?
  How do you crack nuts?

- How does a lion eat meat?
  How do you eat meat?

- How does a bear catch a fish?
  How do you catch a fish?

Research

Go to a library, or online, to help you find answers to these questions:

- What's the difference between a tool and a machine?

- How does an elephant paint?
  How do you paint?

- There are fewer than 10 animals that use tools.
  How many of these animals can you name?
  What "tools" do they use?
  How are they different from the tools a person uses?

Observe

People use tools all the time.

- Watch a grown-up using a tool: write down, or draw, what you see, step-by-step.

The most important tool invented by humans is the wheel.

- When you are outside today, look for wheels. How do the wheels make work easier?

Animals do not use hammers, but people do.

- With an adult's help, use a hammer to tap a nail into some wood. List what you do to use this tool correctly.

What cooking tools do you have in your kitchen?

- Help your grown-up make a meal with the tools that help do the job.

Write, Tell, or Draw

Think about your day.

- What things did you do with your bare hands?
- What things helped you do something that you could not do with your bare hands? List the tools you used.

Imagine a day without any tools such as a toothbrush, a pencil, a fork, spoon, or knife.

- Write about, or tell, what that day would be like.

www.ingramcontent.com/pod-product-compliance
Lightning Source LLC
LaVergne TN
LVHW070837080426
835510LV00026B/3428